THE BALLAD OF BABY DOE

Opera in Two Acts

Music by

DOUGLAS MOORE

Libretto by

JOHN LATOUCHE

Commissioned in honor of the Columbia University Bicentennial by the
Koussevitsky Foundation of the Library of Congress and dedicated
to the memory of Serge and Natalie Koussevitsky.

chappell/intersong
music group–usa

EXCLUSIVELY DISTRIBUTED BY

HAL•LEONARD®
CORPORATION

7777 W. BLUEMOUND RD. P.O. BOX 13819 MILWAUKEE, WI 53213

FOREWORD

The chief characters in "The Ballad of Baby Doe" are drawn from actual figures in American history. Baby Doe, Horace and Augusta Tabor, and their fellow-citizens in Leadville and Denver are recreated from pages of Colorado's fabulous mining era, at the turn of the century. William Jennings Bryan and President Chester A. Arthur, who touch on the story at certain points, reflect the larger American scene as the struggle concerning free gold and silver coinage nearly split the nation asunder.

The dramatic treatment of Tabor's life, and the two women who dominated it, closely follows the pattern of fact. Any shifts in time element and character emphasis have been made to shape the robust chronicle of these lives into the framework of the musical theatre.

The story begins in 1880 at the peak of Tabor's success. After twenty years of poverty, he and his wife, now in their fifties, have attained wealth and power. The classic triangle is formed when Mrs. Elizabeth Doe, known to the miners of Central City as Baby, leaves her husband, Harvey Doe, and comes to Leadville to better her fortunes.

What begins as a flirtation, ends as a deep and abiding love for the man thirty years her senior. But the price of this love is ruin for Tabor. Baby Doe remained true to his memory, however. In 1935, she froze to death at the Matchless Mine, ending the long vigil she had kept there since Tabor's demise in 1899.

"The Ballad of Baby Doe" was first produced at the Central City Opera House, Central City, Colorado, in July 1956; costumes, settings, and lighting by Donald Oenslager; staged by Hanya Holm and Edward Levy; under the musical direction of Emerson Buckley. The principals were:

> HORACE TABOR: Walter Cassel—Clifford Harvuot
> AUGUSTA: Martha Lipton—Frances Bible
> BABY DOE: Dolores Wilson—Leyna Gabriele
> MAMA McCOURT: Beatrice Krebs
> WILLIAM J. BRYAN: Lawrence Davidson—Norman Treigle

The New York premiere by the N. Y. City Center Opera Company occurred on April 3, 1958, staged by Vladimir Rosing and conducted by Emerson Buckley. The principals were:

> HORACE TABOR: Walter Cassel
> AUGUSTA: Martha Lipton
> BABY DOE: Beverly Sills
> MAMA McCOURT: Beatrice Krebs
> WILLIAM J. BRYAN: Joshua Hecht

Cast of Characters

HORACE TABOR, mayor of Leadville . . . . Baritone

AUGUSTA, wife of Horace Tabor . . . . Mezzo-soprano

MRS. ELIZABETH (Baby) DOE, a miner's wife . . . . Lyric Soprano

MAMA McCOURT, Baby Doe's mother . . . . Contralto

WILLIAM JENNINGS BRYAN, candidate for President . . . . Bass baritone

*CHESTER A. ARTHUR, President of the United States . . . . Tenor
FATHER CHAPELLE, priest at the wedding . . . . Tenor
An old silver miner . . . . Tenor
A clerk at the Clarendon Hotel . . . . Tenor
Mayor of Leadville . . . . Tenor
Stage doorman of the Tabor Grand . . . . Tenor

**Bouncer . . . . Baritone
ALBERT, a bellboy . . . . Baritone
A footman . . . . Baritone
A Denver politician . . . . Baritone

SARAH, MARY, EMILY, EFFIE, old friends of Augusta . . . . 2 Sopranos, 2 Mezzo-sopranos

SAM, BUSHY, BARNEY, JACOB, cronies and associates of Tabor . . . . . . 2 Tenors, 2 Baritones

Four Washington dandies . . . . 2 Tenors, 2 Baritones

KATE, dance hall entertainer . . . . Soprano

ELIZABETH, age 12 }
SILVER DOLLAR, age 7 } children of Horace and Baby Doe Tabor . . . . } soprano part / silent part

**MEG, dance hall entertainer . . . . Mezzo-soprano
SILVER DOLLAR (grown up) . . . . Mezzo-soprano
SAMANTHA, a maid . . . . Mezzo-soprano

Dance hall girls, Baby Doe's family, and foreign diplomats at the wedding, miners and their wives

---

*These parts may be covered with two singers.
**These parts may be covered with one singer.

Synopsis of Scenes

ACT I.

Scene 1: Outside the Tabor Opera House, Leadville, 1880.

Scene 2: Outside the Clarendon Hotel, later that evening.

Scene 3: The Tabor apartment, several months later.

Scene 4: The lobby of the Clarendon Hotel, shortly thereafter.

Scene 5: Augusta's parlor in Denver, a year later.

Scene 6: A suite in the Willard Hotel, Washington, D.C., 1883.

ACT II.

Scene 1: The Windsor Hotel, Denver, 1893.

Scene 2: A Club Room in Denver, 1895.

Scene 3: The Matchless Mine, 1896.

Scene 4: Augusta's parlor, November, 1896.

Scene 5: The stage of the Tabor Grand Theatre, April, 1899.

Instrumentation

Flute I	Trombones I-II
Flute II/Piccolo	Tuba
Oboe	Timpani
Clarinets in B♭ I-II	Percussion
Bassoon	Harp
Horns in F I-II	Piano
Trumpets in B♭ I-II	Strings

Applications for performance of this work, whether legitimate, stock, amateur, or foreign, should be addressed to:
TAMS-WITMARK
560 Lexington Avenue
New York, NY 10022

THE BALLAD OF BABY DOE

Libretto by
JOHN LATOUCHE

Act One
Scene One

Music by
DOUGLAS MOORE

The exterior of the Tabor Opera House in Leadville, Colorado. It is not a very big building, but it strains toward grandeur in a timid, rural way. To one side can be seen part of the façade of a saloon. On the other side, the entrance to a hotel is indicated.

As the curtain rises the exterior of the Tabor Opera House is seen. Stage left shows the Clarendon Hotel and on the stage right is a saloon. From the saloon comes the sound of wild shouts and screams mingled with laughter.

Ta - bor loves my Match - less Mine. Go on home and sleep it off. This sa -

loon is Ta-bor's too. Ta-bor owns the op - 'ry house,

Ta - bor owns the big ho - tel. Ta - bor owns this honk - ey tonk,

Ta - bor owns _____ the whole dam town. _____

Girls, shut up! Shut up! And you go home.

Ce - le - bra - tion's o - ver now.

MINER: *f*

Yip - pee!

(14) *The girls, leading the old Miner, throw him about till he's dizzy. The onlookers laugh.*

GIRLS: *f*

Git a - long now to yer

shack and yer dar - ling Clem - en - tine.

(15)

MINER: *f* Onlookers

Ta - bor owns the groc - 'ry store, Ta - bor owns the bank as well. Ta - bor

(Piano)

gradually go offstage and back in saloon.

al - so wants to own My old Match - less

(Trpt.)

p

Andante con moto

It's a bang-up job (If I say it as should-n't) Smart as an-y op-'ry house you're like-ly to see. Chan-de-liers a-glit-ter, Real im-port-ed vel-vet, Brass and ma-hog-a-ny, Tap-es-tries from Eu-rope. Yes-sir, it's a fit-tin' place —— for art and cul-ture. We can stand some cul-ture

TABOR:
here in Col - o - ra - do.

(4 CRONIES:) TENOR 1 & 2:
Lead - ville, Col - o - ra - do!

BARITONE & BASS:
Lead - ville, Col - o - ra - do!

(Fl.)
(Trpt.)

20 SAM (1st CRONY):
Who'd have ev - er thought of it but Hor - ace Ta - bor?

TABOR: mf
You can

Hor - ace Ta - bor

Hor - ace Ta - bor

(Vlns.)

give the cred - it to my wife, Au - gus - ta. She kept on whin - ing This town should have some

(Cl.)

sweet smell-in' dai - sy your - self, Hor-ace Ta-bor, (Strg.) *(pizz.)* Spite of your bear grease and your

(Hn.) *mf*

23 𝅝=𝅗𝅥 *mf*

Flor-i - da wa - ter.___ (Strg.) May - be they call you a loo-ten-ant gov-er-nor.

mf

May - be you struck it rich and own the town of Lead-ville. (Ob.) But to

mf (Hn.)

Bush - y Bar-ney, Sam-u-el and me, you're still a lop eared cut throat from a squat-ter's claim, a

(Strg.) (Fl.Ob.)

(Cl.) *p* *p*

24 SAM, JACOB and CRONIES: *ff* CHORUS (MEN)

fif - ty nin - er min - er, A pan-hand-lin' man, Pan-hand-lin' man!___

f

Allegro con brio

MEN'S CHORUS & CRONIES:

Pan-hand - lin' man!

Fif - ty nin - er min - er out to stake a claim. I came this way from

TABOR:

fine gal is my

Mas - sa - chu - setts through the Kan-sas ter - ri - tor - y, Pick and shov - el in my hand.
wife Au - gus - ta. Nev - er hope to meet a fin - er. Ties me to her a - pron strings

CRONIES & CHORUS:

Bel - ly full of gin and glo - ry. Dig, you go - phers, dig them
Case I dig my way to Chi - na!

holes. Dig a - way to save your souls._____ More buck - ets of
There's ru - bies and

22

Just one eve - ning can't you act with a bit of

dig - ni - ty Can't you man - age to co - op-er - ate in our

ef - forts to pro - vide Some change of

tone in this mon - ey grub - bing town,

Some touch of beau - ty and re - fine -

they work for me   And you owe them some re-

spect.   *poco rit.*   *mf* *a tempo*   Dol - lars__ from that old sa - loon   Same as

(Strgs.)   *a tempo*   *p*   *poco rit.*

46

dol - lars__ from the mines.   Helped to

(Fl. Ob.)   *p*   (Strg.)

build that hand - some op - 'ry house;   Helped to put this__

47

shin - dig on.__   Yep!__

(Trpt.)   (Fl.)   (Cl. Bn.)   (Strg.)   (Vls.)   *p*   (Cl.)

p

⑤⓪

CRONIES: *f*

o - ver now. Let's go in. Yes, my dear, you're

right, you're al - ways right.

*They start to go
back into the
opera house.* *Tabor lingers behind.*

(Piano)

ff
(Hrn.,
Trb.) *f* *rit.*

⑤① **Waltz - Allegro moderato (in 1)**

Baby Doe enters, followed by a Welsh servant. She goes up to Tabor.

mf

BABY:

I beg your par - don. Can you di - rect me to the

⑤②

Clar - en - don Ho - tel? I've just ar -

rived — from Cen - tral Cit - y So I don't know my way — a -

53 bout. Cous - in Jack there knows so lit-tle Eng - - -

poco rit.

lish I have to find the way by my - self. (Vls.) (Cl.)

54 TABOR:
f a tempo

Yon - der is the Clar - en - don And wel - come — to our (Hp.) *f* (Cl. Hn.)

ci - ty. — My name is Hor - ace Ta - bor. If

*If repeat is made 2nd and 3rd beats are played 8va and forte the 1st time.

Scene Two

The exterior of the Clarendon Hotel. Stage left is the entrance of the hotel. Stage right is an outsize window through which a lamp glows. The shades are drawn. Two large windows upstairs also functional, as are the lower door and window. Augusta's friends and Tabor's cronies enter on their way from the concert downstage right. The women wear shawls and carry fans. The men wear capes.

Their voices die away as the light in the large window reveals Baby Doe seated at the piano, playing.

Wil-low, where we met to-geth-er.___ Wil-low, when our love was new.___ Wil-low, if he once should be re-turn-ing, Pray tell him I am weep-ing too. So far___ from each oth-er,___ While the days pass in their emp-ti-ness a-way. Oh my

love, must it be for - ev - er, Nev - er once a - gain to meet as on that

day? And nev - er re - dis - cov - er the way of tell - ing, the way of know - ing

All our hearts would say? Gone are the ways of

pleas - ure Gone are the friends I had of

be re-turn-ing, Pray tell him I am weep-ing too._____ Ah___

Ah_____ Ah_____

Ah_____ Ah___

Ah_____ Ah_____

no one e-ver men-tioned you're still a young man.— A-maz-ing Hor-ace Ta-bor, with

hair like a rav-en's wing.— Eyes a-fire___ with dream-ing like a

boy of sev-en-teen.___

Andante cantabile

TABOR: Warm ___ as the

au-tumn light, Soft ___ as a pool at night, ___ The sound of your

sing - ing, _____ The sound of your sing-ing, Ba - by Doe. _____ And while I was

list' - ning I was re-call - ing Things that

once _ I had want-ed so much _ And for-got-ten as years slipped a -

way. _____ A girl I knew back home in Ver-mont The

sea___ in New Hamp-shire, The first sight___ of the moun - tains.___ They

Piu mosso
77

say___ I've been luck - y;___ there's noth- ing my mon - ey won't buy.___ It

could- n't be I was un - hap - py___ or was miss- ing the good things of

poco rit.   **A tempo primo**

life.___ But on - ly to- night___ came a - gain___ in your

(78)

sing - ing___ That feel - ing of won - der Of

molto rit. **A tempo**

long - ing and pain.___ Deep___ in your love - ly eyes

(W.W.) (Vl.)

(Hn. Trb.)

All___ of en - chant - ment lies_____ And ten - der - ly

cresc.

beck - ons___ And ten - der - ly beck - ons, Ba - by

(Cl. Bn.)

cresc.

TABOR: *Standing very still*

Yes, Au-gus - ta, yes, my dear I am here.___

(Vla.)

(Trb.) (Hn.)

AUGUSTA:

Ar'nt you com-ing up? It's get - ting on to mid - night.

(Vl.) (Fl. Cl.)

(Trpt.)

80 TABOR:

Just as you say, my dear.___

He goes to the door of
the hotel.

cresc. *ff*

An - y thing you say.___

Curtain

cresc. *ff*

(Hn.)

The large, ornate livingroom of a hotel apartment. Samantha, an impassive middleaged maid, is lighting the lamps against the deepening twilight outside.

Augusta moves away from the window as Samantha picks up a turkey feather duster. Augusta has been taking her glasses out of the case.

Più mosso

I sup-pose she's young and pret-ty, Gid-dy too and friv-o-lous to have such slen-der hands.

Samantha nods and leaves quietly. Augusta holds up her hands tragically.

Allegro maestoso

Look at my hands! They're old and red and twist-ed. On them is writ-ten, in ev-'ry ag-ing wrin-kle, the re-cord of the bit-ter years. These hands have worked to help him.

Più mosso - Allegro pesante

Hands rough with work-ing, Cook-ing, scrub-bing, mend-ing. Hands that e-ven

Horace enters and goes straight to the writing desk where he starts rummaging among the papers.

Allegro moderato

(105) AUGUSTA:

What are you look-ing for Hor-ace? Per-haps — I can help you find it. I'm

TABOR:

look-ing for the check — I made out last night, the down

pay-ment — on that mine of Jake's.

(106) AUGUSTA:

The Match-less

TABOR: Mine? — Yes, — the Match-less Mine. —

AUGUSTA: Well, you

Andante con moto

Tabor

She's noth-ing but a strum-pet.

see her all I can. You got no right to say that.

(Fl.) (Ob.)
(Bn.)

119 Meno mosso

Ev-'ry-bod-y talks a-bout her.

rall. mf
Ev-'ry-bod-y's tell-ing lies. She's beau-ti-ful and gen-er-ous.

tr
(Fl. Ob.)
rall. p (Hn.) dolce

All the warmth and ten-der-ness I longed for she has giv-en me. You should be a-shamed of the

cold-ness which di-vides us. What's the use of liv-ing like you're al-read-y dead?

f rit.
f rit.

The lobby of the Clarendon Hotel. Stage right a staircase is partly seen ascending straight up to the second floor. Beside stands the clerk's desk, with the clerk busy at his register and accounts.
Stage left a row of chairs and an exit to the street. Down stage left, a writing desk with stationery and quill pen in evidence. Center stage, a circular bench with potted palm in the center.

the stairs with a bell boy following her, carrying her bags. She carries a hatbox and is adjusting her feather boa as she descends. CLERK: mf

Why Miss - us Doe,___ You can't be think-ing of leav - ing us so

He turns to
the guests.

bout to leave Lead-ville. If he comes back and finds her gone he'll skin us both a-live.

(132) *Poco meno* *Allegro moderato*

Sor - ry to keep you wait - ing. Right this way, I'll show you to your rooms.

The clerk seizes a key from the rack and darts out. The stodgy elderly couple follow, staring at each other in faint surprise.

BABY: *(Writing)*

(133)

Dear-est Ma - ma, I am writ - ing, For I'm lone - ly and dis -

tressed. I am stay - ing here in Lead - ville with-out Har - vey, by my-

But, dear ma - ma he's not free to mar - ry. It is wrong for us to feel the way we do. I know he needs me and that I love him, But I have to give him up and we must part for - ev - er, for - e ver, for - e - ver.

Baby Doe reads over the letter.

Allegro moderato

She sighs and signs it.

BABY: *p*

Your lov-ing daugh-ter Liz-zie.

(137A) Allegro non troppo

colla voce

ff

Augusta appears at the head of the stairs. She sees Baby alone at the writing desk.

She approaches her firmly.

Più mosso

(138)

AUGUSTA: *mf*

Ex-cuse me, but arn't you Mis-sus Har-vey

BABY: *p*

Doe?___ Yes,___ I am.___

(139) AUGUSTA: *mf*

I'm Au-gust-a Ta-bor,

Please be-lieve me, that was all! _____ I'm not good at_

judg - ing__ peo - ple. Live and let live is my__ mot - to.

Have a good time if you can But how can one judge, _____ or

ques - tion, or doubt for a mo - ment, A man of such great - ness? Un-

us - u - al men all have un - us - u - al ways _____ All we can

do _____ is to try to be wor - thy. That is our du -

ty. That is our priv - i - lege. ___ Now I am leav - ing,

Miss - us Ta - bor. But I beg you try to un - der -

stand _____ He must be free _____ to fol - low his

des - ti - ny, For he is a - bove ___ all con - ven - tion - al ways. ___

Scene Five

Augusta's parlor. Augusta is seated in a high back chair. Clustering about her are four agitated women - her friends.

(189) Piu mosso

off.

Tell the truth, Tell the truth. Shout it from the house-tops,

(Hn.) trem.

(Cl.)

Shout it from the house-tops. De - cent wo - men ev - ery-where will

(Vl.)

Augusta rises Maestoso

If he ev - er tries to di -

ral - ly by your side

(Trpt.) (Trb.)

(Hn.)

(190)

vorce me, I'll make him rue

Scene Six
Finale - Act One

A private room in the old Willard Hotel, Washington. The room, a dream of marble pillars, stately fireplaces, old plush carpets, is garlanded with flowers. Stage left, there is a table heaped with flowers and presents, its center piece is six feet high—"a wedding-bell of white roses surmounted by a heart of red roses, which is pierced by an arrow of violets, shot from a Cupid's bow of heliotrope".

The chief entrance to the room, rear center stage, is elevated by a stairway at least six steps high, so that a dramatic or dawdling descent may be made on it.

As the curtain rises, Mrs. McCourt is rushing around the room, arranging the flowers. Mr. McCourt, his son and daughter (with spouses if possible) are sitting uncomfortably on the gilt chairs to one side of the room.

A group of four Dandies (doubtless from the State Department) stand apart and aloof.

DANDIES:

High pro-tec-tive rates are hurt-ing trade o-ver-seas. Eng-land, France and Ger-ma-ny

High pro - tec-tive rates are hurt-ing trade. Eng-land, France and Ger-ma-ny

All are e-rect-ing re-tal-i-a-tive bar-ri-ers A-

All are e-rect-ing re-tal-i-a-tive bar-ri-ers So that they dis-crim-i-nate a-

cresc.

cresc.

Fl.

(196)

Mama listens vaguely, then goes to the door to greet new arrivals.

gainst A-mer - i-can raw pro - ducts.

gainst A-mer - i-can raw pro - ducts.

(Fl.)

MAMA

Yes,

was-n't Liz - zie a love-ly blush-ing bride? And Ta-bor

(197)

made a strik-ing fig-ure as well. Ain't they a love - ly

cou - ple?

PAPA and FAMILY: *mf*

A love - ly, love - ly cou - ple.

CHORUS:

A

A

114

on these oc - ca - sions And one al - ways says:___ you hav - n't

lost _____ a daugh - ter, You have on - ly

gained _____ a son.

FAMILY: *f*
That's what we all have

told her. _____

SOPRANO: *f*
ALTO: Yes, you must think of it that way! _____
TENOR: *f*
BASS: Yes, you must think of it that way! _____

PRIEST: *mf*
You are

GUESTS:

doub - ly blest in such a lov - ing cou - ple.___

(Fl.)
(Ob.)

(Hn.)

(205)

GUESTS:
Lov - ing ___ Cou - ple.

Lov - ing ___ Cou - ple.

(Trpt.)
(Octs.)

rall.

*The rear center doors open and the footman
steps forward and announces —*
FOOTMAN: The Senator and Mrs. Horace
Tabor.

CHORUS:
Here they come, Here they come! ___

Here they come, Here they come! ___

(Vl.)
(Trpts.)

molto rit.
trem.

rall.

Tabor enters with Baby Doe on his arm. She is dressed ravishingly; he is a bit uncomfortable in white tie, but is feeling expansive.

*The chief Dandy kisses
her hand and the others
gather about her.*

dreams

Andante molto moderato

TABOR: And I'll show you some-thing else that sil - ver can do.

It can buy you gold and dia - monds or an - y-thing you please.

(216) *Clasps his hands.* **Allegro moderato** *A servant steps forward with a velvet case*

For ex - am - ple: Boy!

For

He puts the jewels on Baby and the guests gasp in admiration.

of the U - ni-ted States, Hon-'ra-ble Ches-ter A. Ar - thur.

Allegro brillante   *The President bustles in cheerfully, followed by two Naval aides.*

The crowd turns back as he kisses Baby Doe's hand.

PRESIDENT: *mf*

I'm

sor - ry —— to be late, my dear. You're not too

late, You're just in time, Ches - ter,

He claps the President on the back.

End of Act One

Act Two
(Scene One)

The Governor's Ball. 1893.   A balcony off the Ballroom of the Windsor Hotel.

Tempo di Valse

Piano

Curtain.
Through the lighted windows dancers can be seen moving to the rhythm of a gay Polka. Augusta's four friends come out

Allegretto poco andante

1st FRIEND:
Well! the ef - front-er - y of that wo-man!

2nd FRIEND: *f*
Ba - by Doe Ta - bor,

4th FRIEND: *mf*
Ta - bor in-deed! Done up like a Christ-mas tree,

3rd FRIEND:
Mak-ing big eyes at

1st FRIEND: *mf*
He

1st & 2nd CRONIES: *mf*
high up in the par - ty. Next time he may be chos - en gov - er - nor.

250
nev - er will be gov - er - nor with Ba - by as his wife.

3rd FRIEND:
1st & 2nd FRIENDS
He nev - er will with

2nd FRIEND: *mf*
No, he nev - er will

3rd & 4th FRIENDS:
with

3rd CRONY: *f*
Ba - by as his wife. Come off of it, girls, she's made a good wife

Ba - by as his wife.

4th CRONY: *mf*
And moth - er to his

(Cl.)

(Trb.) *f* (Hn.) *p* (Bn.) ⁊

(252)

Baby Doe comes out on the balcony, followed by Mama.

Tempo di Valse   THE MEN: Sh-h-h   BABY: *Fanning herself*

She sees the men.

How are you, boys!____ Good eve - ning,

la - dies. Good eve - ning one and all. Is - n't it a love - ly

The friends turn their backs on her and go inside, followed reluctantly by the cronies.

par - ty?____

My, it's chill - i - er in here than I thought. Those

Atempo primo

let _____ them sneer _____ and pass me by, As they

264A

look down their nos - es at me. _____

I have a love that will keep me a - glow as the world grows

264B

gray and cold _____ And that is

more than they ev - er will know. If they did

they would be kind _____ But they nev - er,

nev - er, nev - er will know; They nev - er will

know. _____

265 Allegro

A butler comes in stage left with a card on a tray.

Baby looks

at the card, nods to the butler, who withdraws.

(266) BABY: Ma-ma, go in-side and find Hor-ace. Tell him to come here. Tell him quick-ly.

(Vla.)

(Vl.)

Mama rushes off along the balcony. incalzando

accel. (Cl.) cresc.

(Hn.)

(267)

Augusta enters, austere in a black ballgown.

Maestoso

The two women bow

(Ob.) (Vl.)

(Cl.) (Hn.)

AUGUSTA: p

Mis-sus Ta-bor, I go out rare-ly, But when the

(Fl.)

dim.

pp (Strg.)

gov - er - nor an-nounced a ball to ho - nor Hor - ace, I thought I

might at - tend. Am I wel-come? There is some-thing I must say. If

Allegro ma non troppo

you have come in an - ger, There is noth - ing to

say. You've had your sat - is - fac - tion of me; Your friends have seen to

that. All these years ___ not one of them Has o - pened a door to

Baby makes an impulsive gesture towards her.

BABY: *p*

love is free-dom and they fear it.

I tru-ly re-pent an-y wrong I did you.

AUGUSTA: *p*

The wrong was done long be-fore you came.— I too— feared love's free-dom. Now I am

old— and ill. I have learned this too late And must die in the pris-on— of my-self a-

for-tune is on pa-per. Ev-'ry-one knows that the

price of sil-ver Is half what it was ten years a-

go._____ But still I read of noth-ing

But his ex-trav-a-ganc-es. BABY: *p* His

277 *calando* *poco rall.* AUGUSTA: *p*

mon-ey run-ning out? He nev-er told me. He would

(281)

you do-ing here? Is it not e-nough to turn

half the town a-gainst me, Must you turn my dar-ling a-

gainst me as well? BABY: *mf dim.* Hor-ace, you

don't un-der-stand, Hor-ace! Meno mosso TABOR: *mf* Sell the Match-less

(282) Mine she says. It's made you rich e-nough, has-n't it, Au-

AUGUSTA: gus-ta? Hor-ace, it's too late for an-ger be-tween us.

BABY: Don't turn me a-way. Tru-ly, she came in kind-ness.

(283) **Allegro moderato**

TABOR: The kind-est thing that she can do Is to leave us in peace. Who asked her here, With all this talk of ru-in? I want

Scene Two
A Club Room in Denver 1895

In a cone of light from a hanging lamp, the green felt of a circular gaming table is stacked with poker chips, and splashed with playing cards. Tabor's four cronies are around the table in their shirt sleeves playing poker. As the light comes on they are intent on the game.

174

(2913)

Scene Three

A sunny afternoon in 1896. The exterior of the Matchless Mine. The mine itself (which will be seen in a stark simplicity in the epilogue) is now hidden behind scaffolding and bleachers. The miners' wives are decorating the scaffolding with bunting as the curtain rises.

The center stage scaffolding is a speaker's stand, which is furnished with a lectern. The base of the lectern is adorned with a hugh photograph of William Jennings Bryan. Below the photograph are the glowing initials: W. J. B. Other banners proclaim -"Welcome to Bryan", etc.

The miners' wives are singing as they beautify the scene. They should be heard before the rise of the curtain.

Baby Doe enters, followed by her two children and her mother. She is dressed plainly.

Allegretto marziale

BABY: tru - ly. When Mis-ter Bry-an makes a speech, ev-'ry-bod-y list-ens. Be-

cause, when he speaks, It is ev-'ry-bod-y talk-ing. And

so, he is the wis-est man. So, he is the great-est man. And

OLDER GIRL: Ex - cept dad-dy! Ex-

(298) So, he is the best man in the whole U. S A.

cept dad-dy. Ex-

BABY and the WOMEN:
"They're coming, they're coming."

pres - i - dent of this our might - y coun - try!

pres - i - dent of this our might - y coun - try!

(Picc. & Trpt.)
soli

ff

(Bass Dr.)

etc.

300

(Trpt.)
(Trb.)

"Hooray" etc.

Shouting and cheering off stage

(Tutti)

Tabor comes in at the head of the procession.

As Tabor moves to the platform he exhorts the crowd.

TABOR:

You

(301) Allegro giusto

min - ers, doc - tors and you cow-pokes, You cit - y sharps and farm - ing

(Timp.)

folks,_____ You're not deaf and dumb and blind. Now it's time to speak your mind.

(302)

MEN CHORUS:* f

Tell it to the na - tion Up - on e - lec - tion day! We're not deaf and

(Hn. Tuba) mf

dumb and blind. Now it's time to speak our minds And we'll speak it

(303)

next e - lec - tion day. Ev' - ry - bod - y'd bet - ter lis - ten 'cause we got a

9471 *If the Men's Chorus is small, parts should be doubled by women's voices 8va.

Tabor goes offstage for a moment and returns with W.J. Bryan and the Mayor. The three greet some of the people and mount the speaker's platform.

WOMEN
CHORUS
MEN

Vote for Bry - an, Doub - le - U - J - B, 'Cause he can't be bought and he

Vote for Bry - an, Doub - le - U - J - B, 'Cause he can't be bought and he

(Brass)

can't be sold And he won't nail us to a cross of gold. Sil - ver Dol - lar

can't be sold And he won't nail us to a cross of gold. Sil - ver Dol - lar

Sez "in God we Trust", So it's Bry - an we will fol - ler as Mc - Kin - ley

Sez "in God we Trust", So it's Bry - an we will fol - ler as Mc - Kin - ley

(Trb.)

bites the dust. Bry - an, Bry - an, Bry - an, Bry - an, Bry - an, Bry - an,

bites the dust. Bry - an, Bry - an, Bry - an, Bry - an, Bry - an, Bry - an,

9471

MAYOR: *(on platform attempting to introduce Bryan.)*

The mayor gives up with a shrug and motions Bryan to begin. He silences the crowd with a sweeping gesture.

Bry - an. _____ Crowd breaks into cheers.

Bry - an.

BRYAN:
Good peo-ple of Lead-ville, I beg of you to think of me ___ as one of your-selves ___ And to for - bear ap-plause ___ for the hum-blest cit-i-zen in all the land When clad in the ar-mor of a right-eous cause is strong-er than all the hosts of er - ror. Ours is a cause as ho - ly as the cause of lib-er-ty it-self.

The child waits patiently beside him with the bunch of roses.

depths of earth to find there gleam-ing sil - ver, You are the sin-ews of our na - tion's strength.

(Cl.)

(Hp.)

(Hn.)

316

You har - dy pi - o - neers, who have made the de - sert to blos - som like the

(Fl.)

(Cl.2)

The child tugs at his coatails. *He sees the child. She curtsies low and hands him the roses.*

rose Thank you my dear for this un - ex-pect-ed trib-ute.

ad lib

(Solo Vl.)

espress.

She grins at the crowd shyly and whispers in his ear.

What's your name, child? Well, Miss Ta-bor, your fa - ther is rich in -

(Fl.)

pp espress.

He addresses the crowd.

317 **Andante maestoso**

deed to num - ber you a - mong his pos - ses - sions. Take Hor-ace

(Vl.)

mf

(Hn.)

Ta - bor now, Leg - is - la - tion made him poor. But no

laws can break his spir - it, fight - ing here be-side us And our com - mon

318

cause is sil - ver Let this love - ly in - no - cent serve as your sym - bol.

Broad

He reaches into one of the bags of ore banked about the lectern.

rall. molto

She laughs, brushes the dust from her

Child, I chris - ten thee "Sil - ver Dol - lar."

hair and hides her face in Bryan's coat. Tabor steps forward and takes her from Bryan's arms.

p a tempo

Come, let us build ___ a fair - er E - den Up - on this

9471

Molto più mosso

203

322

marching to glory with our faces to the sky. All enemies we put to rout.

Come on, throw the rascals out. Listen to the people shout Bry-an!

323

(Shouting)

Bry-an! Bry-an, Bry-an, Bry-an, Bry-an, Foe of the wicked and com-

panion of the blest, loyal friend of the people And the savior of the West.

Come cit - i - zens and join our band Rise up joy - ful in the land March-ing on to vic - to - ry with

Come cit - i - zens and join our band Rise up joy - ful in the land March-ing on to vic - to - ry with

Some of the men raise Bryan on their shoulders.

rall.

a tempo

Bry - an — To glo - ry and to vic - to - ry with Bry -

Bry - an — To glo - ry and to vic - to - ry with Bry -

rall.

a tempo

324

Curtain

an.

Wild cheering and shouting.

an.

(Timp.)

ff

Allegro maestoso

(Cl.)

(Trpt.)
(Trb.) *ff*   (Hn.)

(Picc.)
Fl.

dim. e allarg.

(Timp.)

ff

9471

attacca subito

Scene Four

Augusta's Study.   *A few weeks later.*

When the curtain rises
Augusta is standing at the window of her room looking out, listening to the newsboys cry out the news of Bryan's defeat.

Samantha enters (upper left), whispers to Augusta, then admits Mama McCord and goes off.

MAMA: Miss-us Ta-bor, For-give me. What can I do for you? I'm Liz-zie's ma-ma.

AUGUSTA: Yes, I re-mem-ber.

MAMA: I've come here on a sad er-rand.

AUGUSTA: Yes?

MAMA: Ta-bor is pen-ni-less. Bry-an was his last hope. Now that is gone. They're tak-ing

351 Andante appassionato *languido, col angoscia e sempre rubato colla parte*

Ta-bor, my hus-band! Ta-bor, my dear one! Why, why did you ev - er leave me?

Now at last, Now that Ta - bor needs Au - gus - ta, I should go but I am a - fraid.

352 *molto rit.* *a tempo* Allargando molto

mf cresc. Ta-bor once loved me. Once a - gain I hear him call, Call-ing on Au - gust-a, Au-

molto rit. piangendo gust - a. But I can-not go.

Curtain

Act Two
Scene Five

The stage of the Tabor Grand Theater. 1899.

STAGE DOORMAN:
Hey mis-ter! You come back! You ain't got no right in here.

Andante con moto

TABOR:
This is the Ta - bor Grand The - a - ter And I am H. A. Dou - ble - U Ta - bor. Who else has a great - er right To take a bow up - on this stage?

STAGE DOORMAN:
Mis-ter Ta-bor? I'm sor-ry! In this dark,

be like your bro-ther Lem, A hard work-ing god fear-ing man. But

no, you're like your paw, Jack o' Dreams drowned in whis - key.

He tries to embrace her, but she suddenly throws back her bonnet and turns. It is Augusta that we see, but younger and gayer in appearance.

Meno mosso

(366) Slow waltz (in 3)

TABOR. *(Bowing)*
Good af - ter - noon, Miss

AUGUSTA:
Pierce. You may call me Au - gus - ta. We've

TABOR: *mf*

known each oth - er a year now. Au - gus - ta! Au -

(Vl.) *sf* *sf* *sf*

(Bn.)

367

AUGUSTA: *mf*

gus - ta! Named for the cit - y of my birth. How do you like Au -

sf *mf*

TABOR: *p*

gus - ta, Maine? I like the cit - y, but e - ven

cresc.

p **368**

more do I prize its love - ly daugh - ter.

(Fl.) (Vl.)

p (Celeste, Hn.)

M'am, I'm just a stone cut - ter work - ing in your fa - ther's quar - ry.

(Fl.)

(Hp.)

(Cl.)
(Bn.)

But I've got i - deas ___ in my head. ___ I'm goin' to be some-one,

Some - day soon!

Augusta's four friends appear.

AUGUSTA'S FRIENDS:

To be some - one and get some-where You need just

To be some - one and get some-where You need just

AUGUSTA'S FRIENDS: 1, 2, 3, 4

one i - dea: Mar - ry the bos - ses' daugh - ter!

Augusta's friends disappear.

A brief march. Augusta and Tabor join hands and march downstage. Spotlight again falls on politician.

(370) **Allegro maestoso**

AUGUSTA:

prom-ise. You will not squan - der mon - ey.

save your souls. There's_ moun - tains ga - lore of

save your souls. There's_ moun - tains ga - lore of

(Cl.)
p
(Hn.)

A pen-ny saved _____ is a pen-ny earned. I prom-ise.

TABOR: mf

sil - ver_ ore Col - o - ra-do._

sil - ver ore out there in Col - o - ra-do._

f

(372) CRONIES: *A fiddle tune. Stamping feet. The saloon girls come out and dance with the cronies.*

Più mosso

Yip - pee!

(Trpt.)

(Trb.) f

(B.Dr.)

f

Tabor joins them

and swigs from a whiskey bottle.

373

AUGUSTA: Hor - ace! You have bro - ken your prom - ise! TABOR: *rall. e dim.* Yes, my dear.

colla voce *a tempo*

(Ob. Vl.)

(Hn.)

(Timp.)

Trb.

(Light fades out on cronies, saloon girls and Augusta)

Allegro maestoso POLITICIAN:

(Spotlight on Politician) Now, here's the store where he

(Cl.)

(Bn. Vlc.)

(C.B.)

passes so many of his years. Here are the

(374) (Politician light out)
TABOR: (Angrily)

steps of a golden ladder. I tell you I ain't

(S. Dr.)

Miners appear in the shadows.

meant to sit behind a counter toting up figures

(pizz.)

I want to move mountains, rip up the lodes. I ain't no sturdy merchant, I'm a

rit.

rit.
(Trb. Tuba)

Light comes upon miners

un-ion grand of cap-i-tal and la-bor.

un-ion grand of cap-i-tal and la-bor.

Long will the state - ly struc-ture stand, A mon-u-ment to

Long will the state - ly struc-ture stand, A mon-u-ment to

Ta - bor. So fleet, so fleet the works of man. the

Ta - bor. So fleet, so fleet,

works of man. Back to the earth a-gain. An-cient and ho-ly things,

Back to the earth a-gain. An-cient and ho-ly things Fade like a

(Cl.) (Fl.) (Ob.) (Bn.)

rall. mf (380) rall.

feet kicked up gold dust wher-ev-er I danced. And when-ev-er I shout-ed my name I heard a

sil - ver ech-o roar in the wind.

AUGUSTA: Your name will thin like a

whis - per in the wind.

TABOR: There's some-thing-won't let me die, __ Won't let the

dark eat up all of me. __ One thing none can take a - way __ My

Come down moon shine. What will to-mor-row bring? ____

It may bring win-ter and then it may bring spring.

(386)

Me and the weath-er can't get ____ to-geth - er, So keep on

(Vlc.)

mov - ing fast - er, fast - er, fast - er, fast - er,

accel. (She exits) CHORUS: mf cresc.

fast - er, fast - er. Fast - er, fast - er, Fast - er, fast - er.

(Trpt.)

accel. f - p cresc.

*Baby is dressed in a black cloak and a hood which conceals her hair.

Tabor prone. *Baby covers him with her cloak.*

During the first verse the light gradually fades out on Tabor.

eyes. Rest.

pp rall. *a tempo*

The on - ly real thing.

(Vl.)

rall. *a tempo* *p espress.*

p Andante tranquillo

Al - ways through the chang - ing of

p (Hn.) *dolce*

(394)

sun and shad - ow, time and space, I will walk be - side my

love in a green and qui - et place.

mf

Proof a - gainst the forms of fear, No dis - tress shall

(Hp.) *mf* *mf*

eyes grow dim   Still the old_ song_ will be_ sung. I shall

change a - long with him,   So that both _____ are

400 *She is standing in front of the shaft.*

ev - er young, _____   Ev - er

(W.W.) *pp*   (Hn.)

rall.   *Curtain*

young. _____

(Strg.)   *rall.*   (Hn.)

End of Opera